Customer Service: 1-877-277-9441 or customerservice@pikidsmedia.com

Published by Phoenix International Publications, Inc.
8501 West Higgins Road   59 Gloucester Place
Chicago, Illinois 60631   London W1U 8JJ

PI Kids and *we make books come alive* are trademarks of Phoenix International Publications, Inc., and are registered in the United States.

www.pikidsmedia.com

8 7 6 5 4 3 2 1

ISBN: 978-1-5037-5247-4

A Loveliness of Ladybugs

Collective Animal Nouns and the Meanings Behind Them

Written by Kathy Broderick
Illustrated by Gabriele Tafuni

we make books come alive®
pi **Phoenix International Publications, Inc.**
Chicago • London • New York • Hamburg • Mexico City • Sydney

a loveliness
of ladybugs

loveliness \LUV-lee-nuss\ *noun* : the qualities in a person or
thing that as a whole give pleasure to the senses

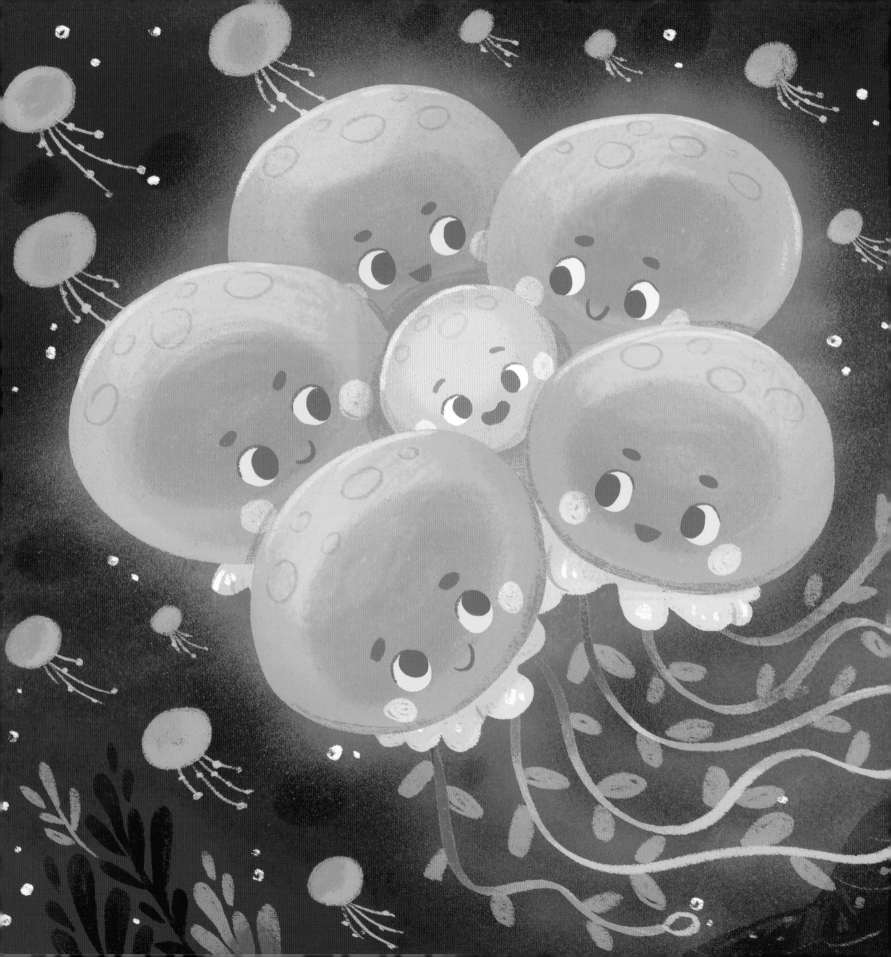

a bloom
of jellyfish

bloom \BLOOM\ *verb* : to produce flowers

a prickle of porcupines

prickle \PRIK-ul\ *noun* : a prickling or tingling sensation

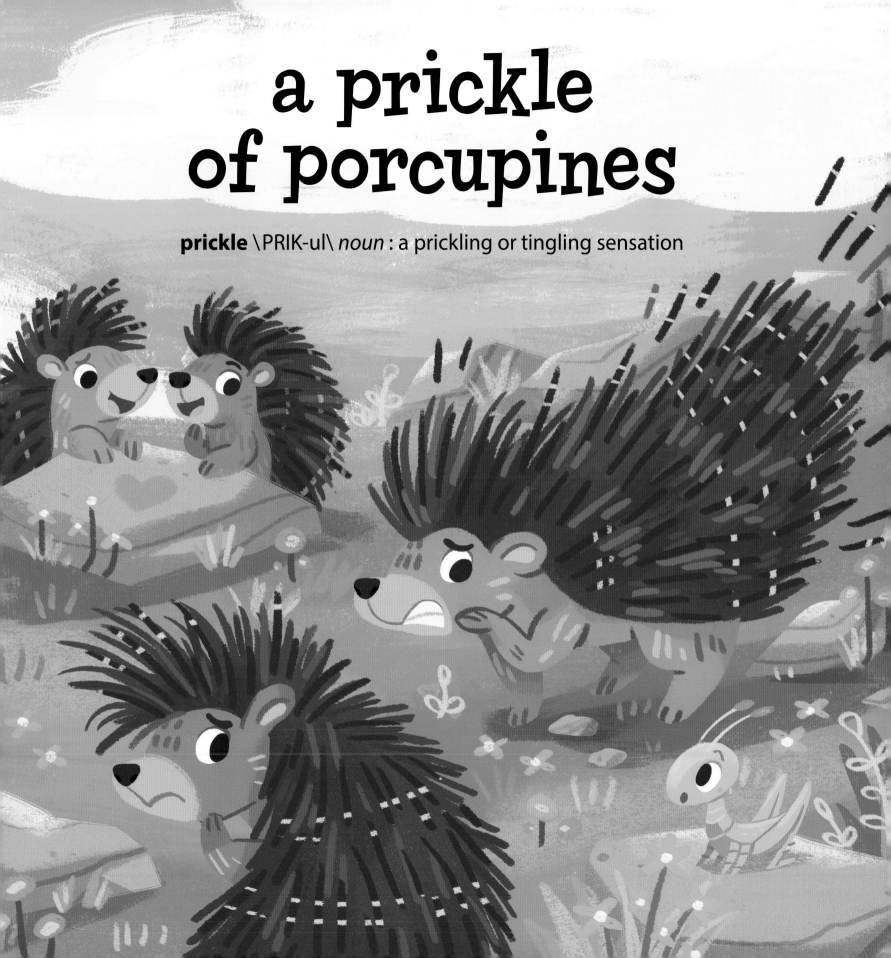

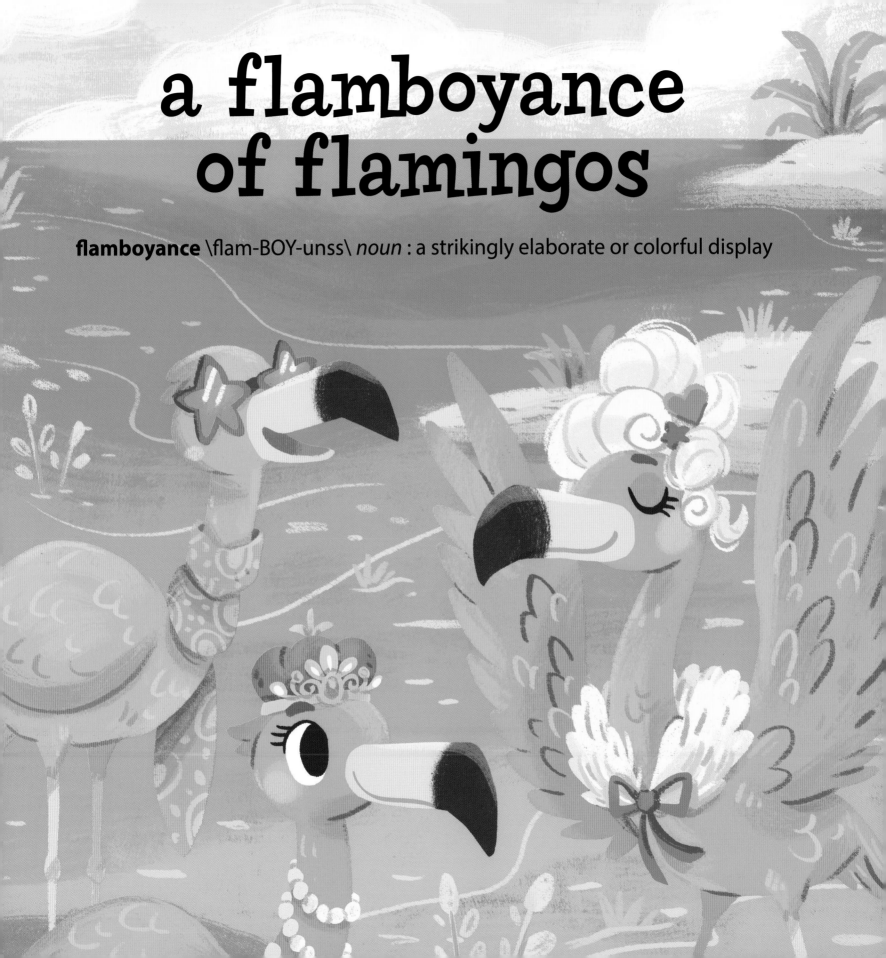

a flamboyance
of flamingos

flamboyance \flam-BOY-unss\ *noun* : a strikingly elaborate or colorful display

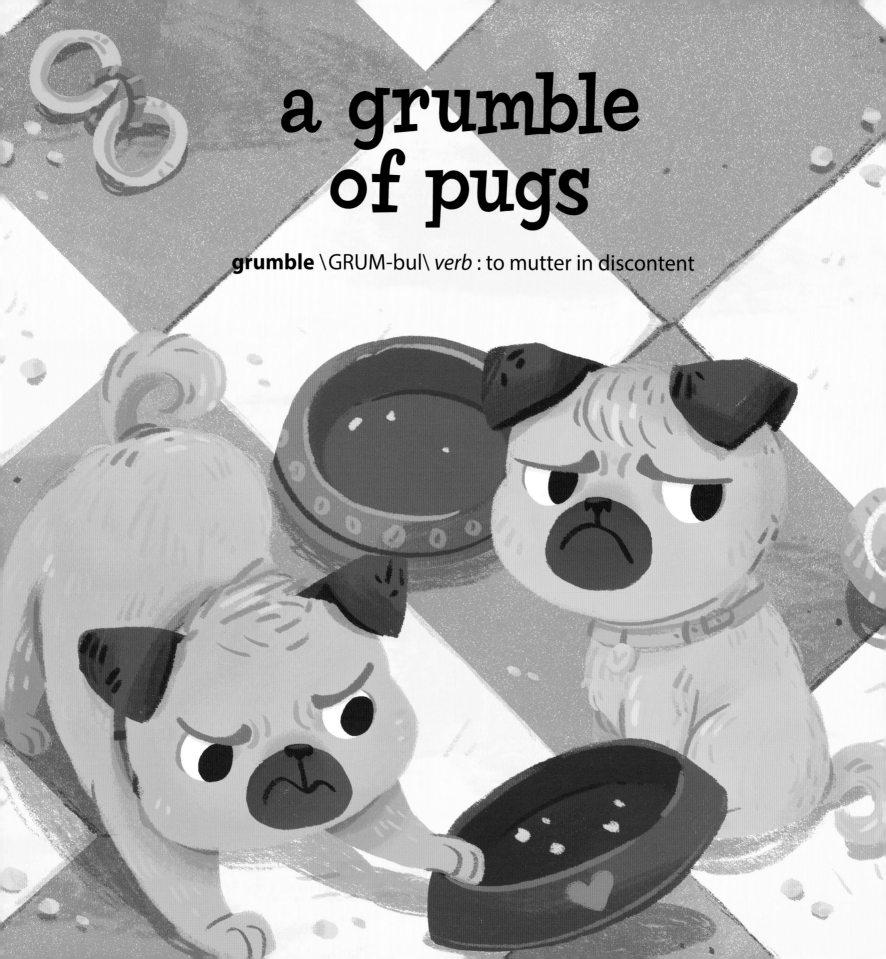

a grumble of pugs

grumble \GRUM-bul\ *verb* : to mutter in discontent

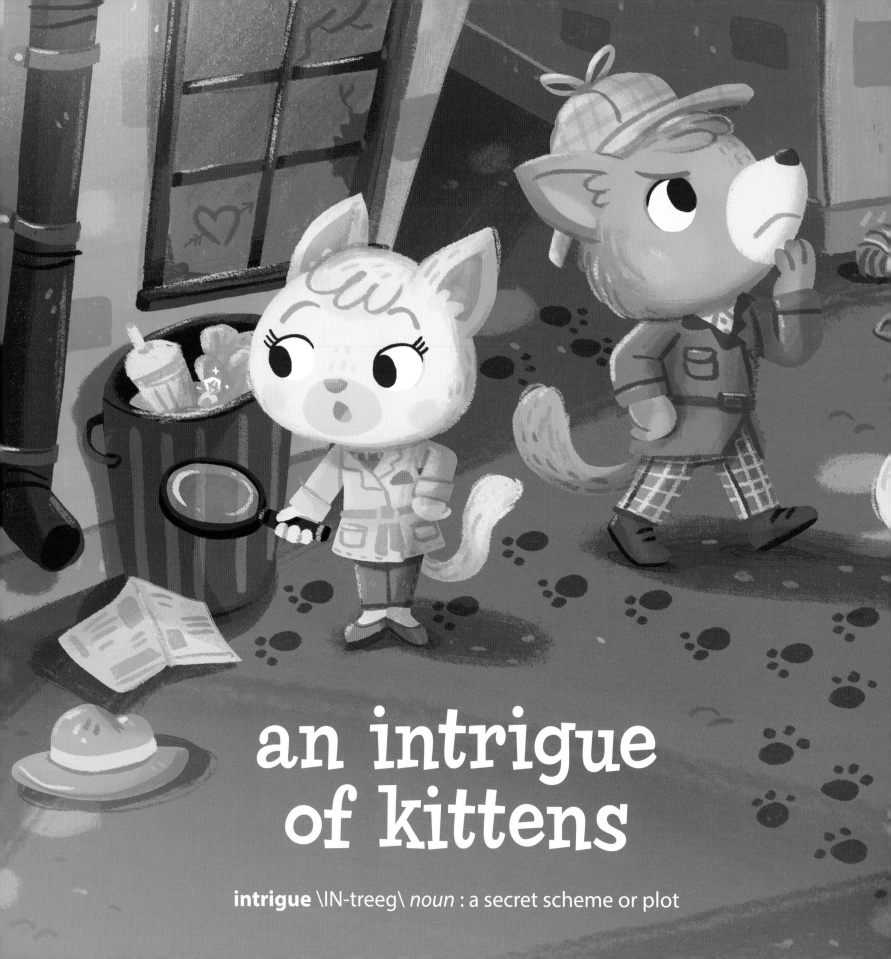

an intrigue of kittens

intrigue \IN-treeg\ *noun* : a secret scheme or plot

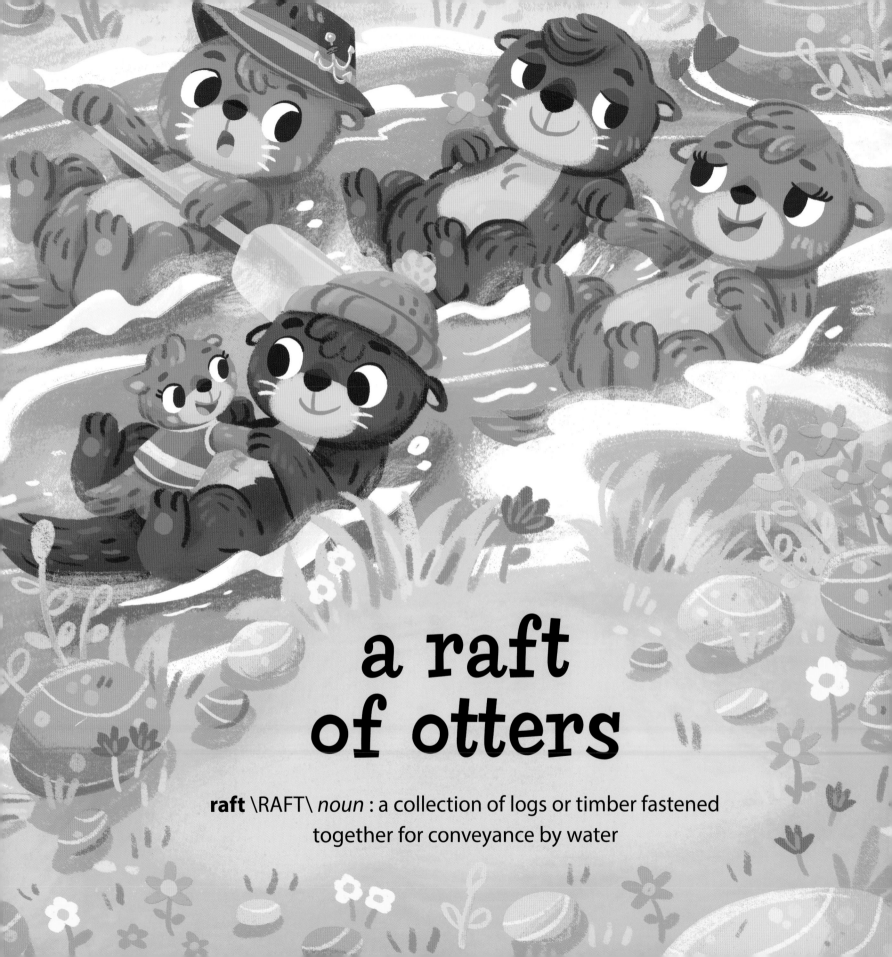

a raft of otters

raft \RAFT\ *noun* : a collection of logs or timber fastened together for conveyance by water

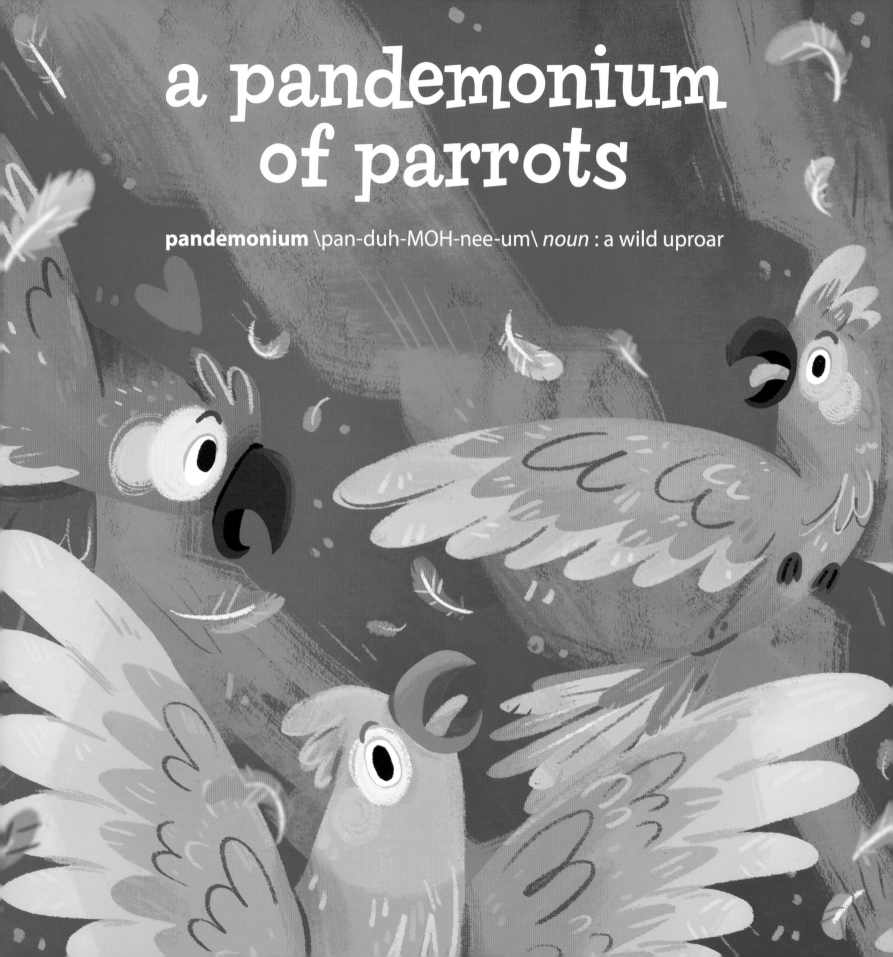

a pandemonium
of parrots

pandemonium \pan-duh-MOH-nee-um\ *noun* : a wild uproar

a shiver
of sharks

shiver \SHIV-er\ *noun* : an intense shivery sensation,
especially of fear

a waddle of penguins

waddle \WAH-dul\ *verb* : to walk with short steps swinging the forepart of the body from side to side

a kaleidoscope of butterflies

kaleidoscope \kuh-LYE-duh-skohp\ *noun* : a tube that contains bits of colored glass or plastic and two mirrors at one end and that shows many different patterns as it is turned

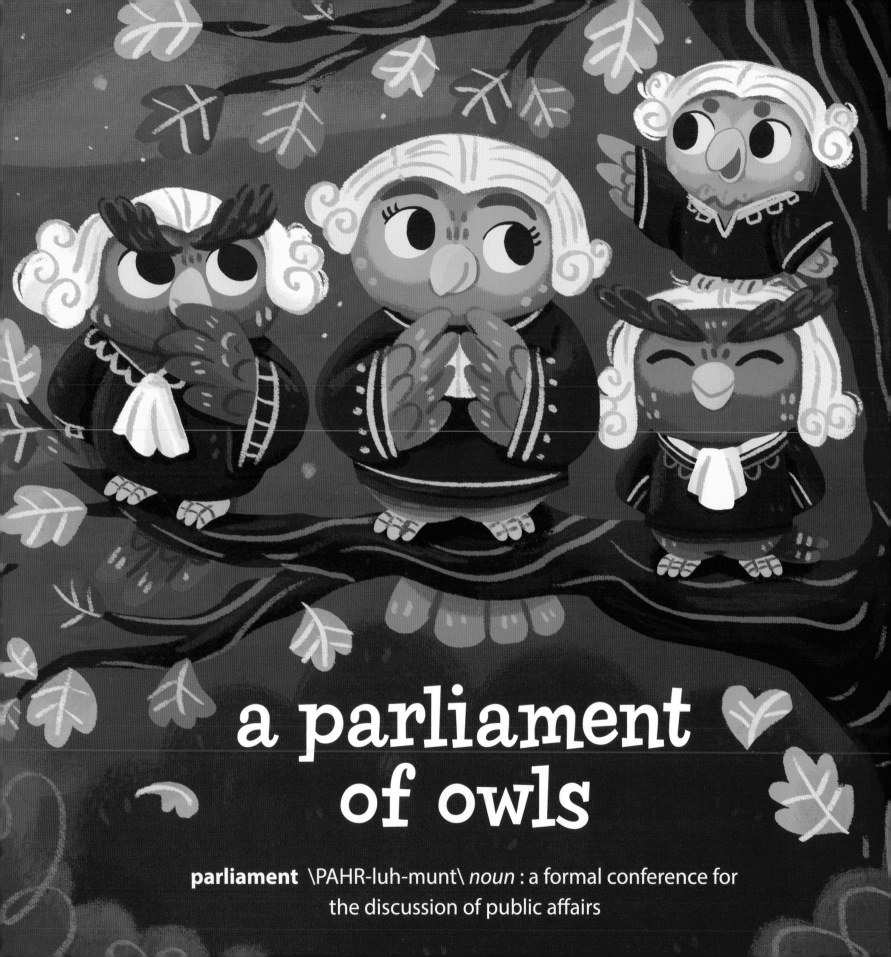

a parliament of owls

parliament \PAHR-luh-munt\ *noun* : a formal conference for the discussion of public affairs

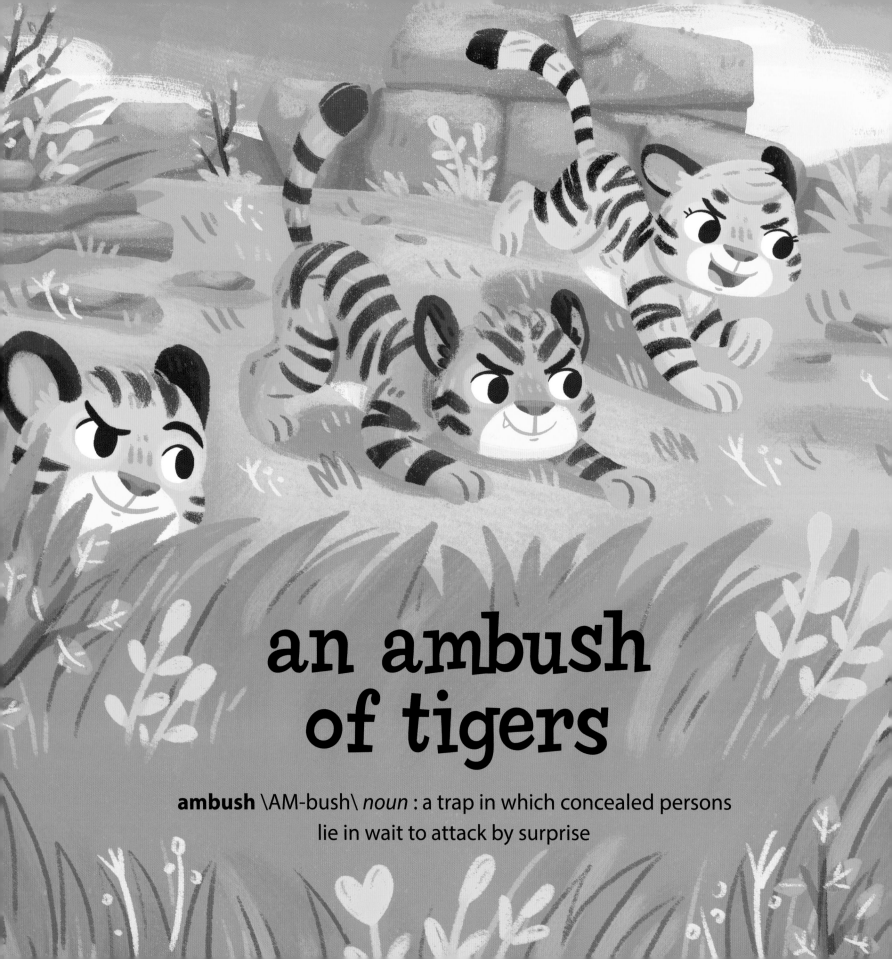

an ambush of tigers

ambush \AM-bush\ *noun* : a trap in which concealed persons lie in wait to attack by surprise

an ostentation of peacocks

ostentation \ah-stun-TAY-shun\ *noun* : an excessive display

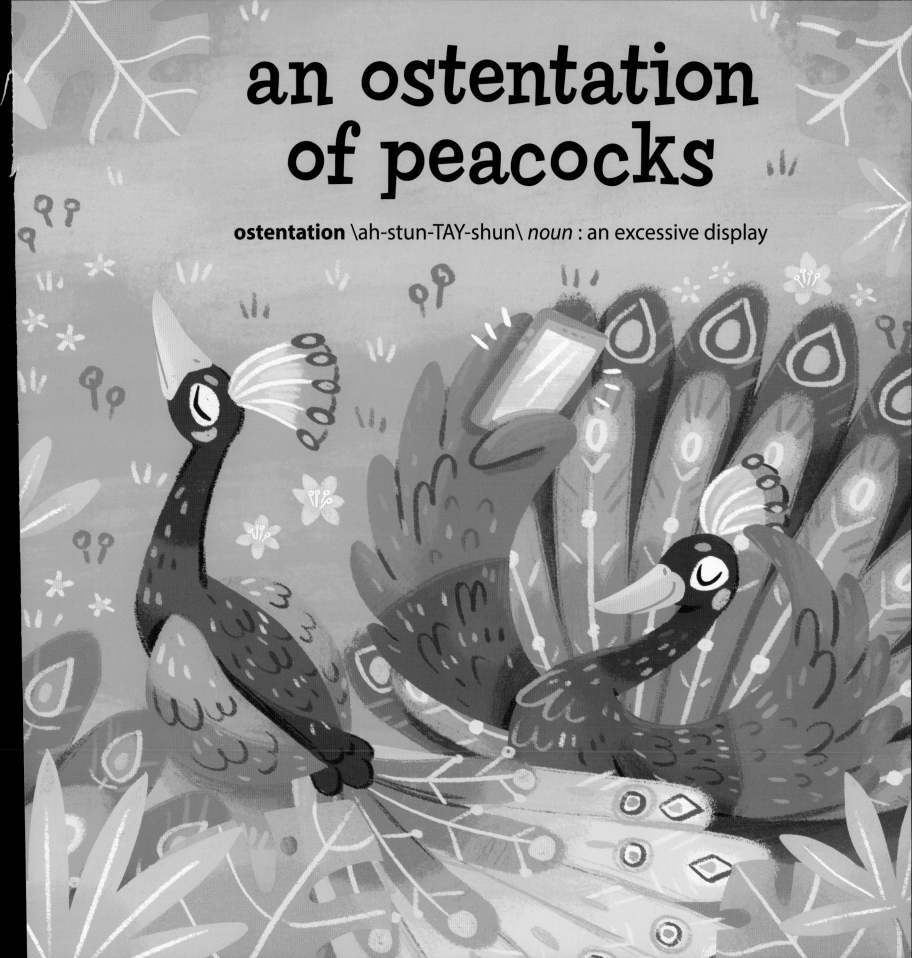

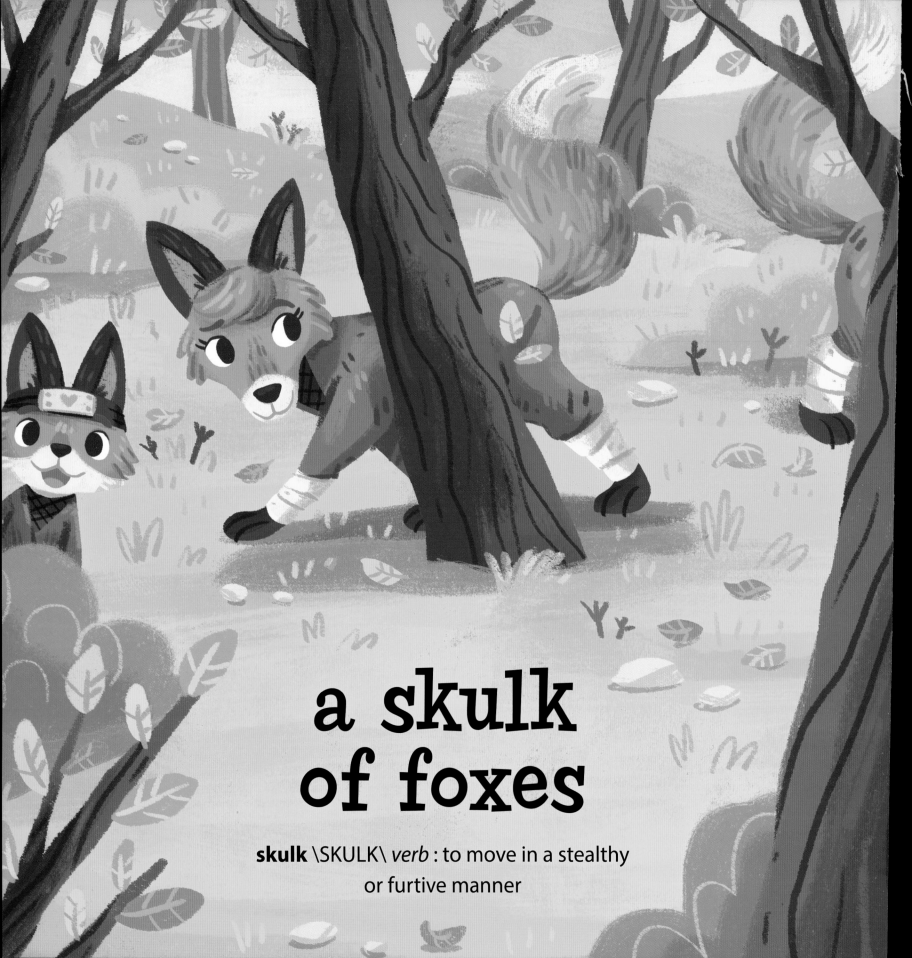

a skulk
of foxes

skulk \SKULK\ *verb* : to move in a stealthy
or furtive manner

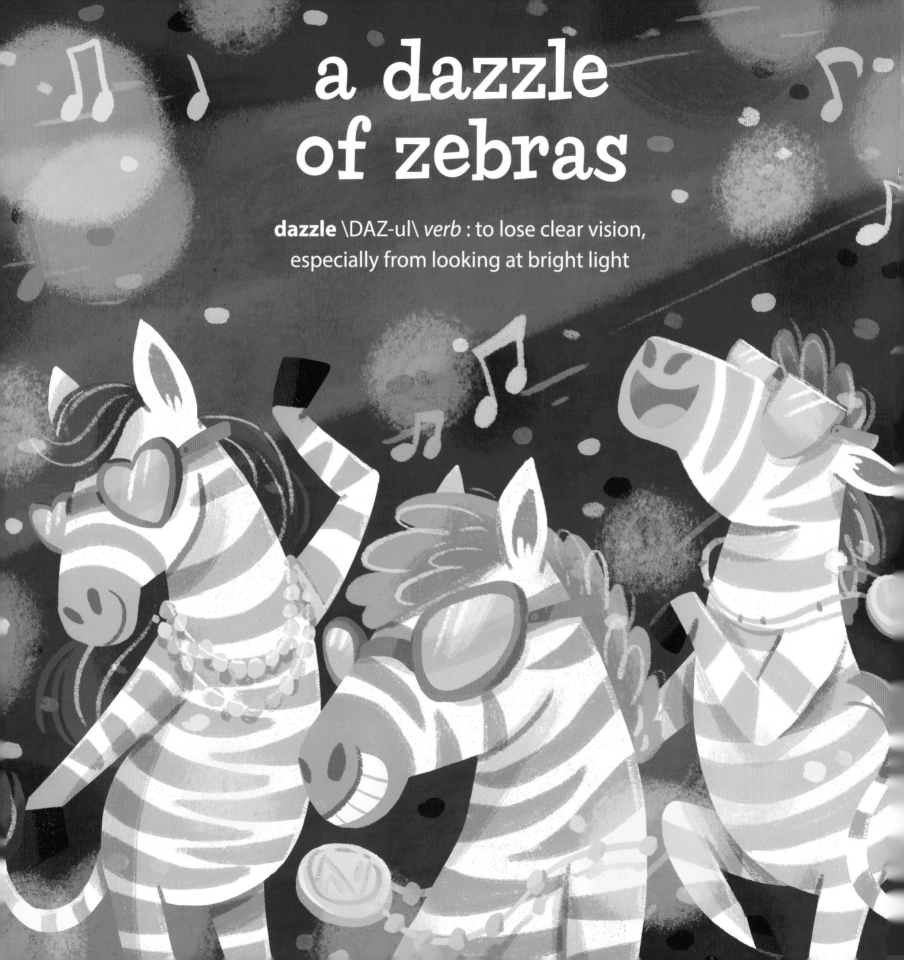

a dazzle of zebras

dazzle \DAZ-ul\ *verb* : to lose clear vision, especially from looking at bright light